To

_____

From

_____

Date

_____

B

A TREASURY OF PRAYERS FOR

Every Occasion

TIMELESS
BLESSINGS

Ellie Claire

gift & paper expressions

...inspired by life

EllieClaire.com

Ellie Claire™ Gift & Paper Expressions
Brentwood, TN 37027
EllieClaire.com

Timeless Blessings
Prayers and Blessings for Every Occasion
© 2014 by Ellie Claire, an imprint of Worthy Media, Inc.

ISBN 978-1-60936-937-8

Stock or custom editions of Ellie Claire titles may be purchased in bulk for educational, business, ministry, fundraising, or sales promotional use. For information, please e-mail info@EllieClaire.com

Compiled by Jill Olson.
Cover and interior design by Gearbox | studiogearbox.com

Printed in China.

1 2 3 4 5 6 7 8 9 – 19 18 17 16 15 14

Contents

Praises and blessings. Invocations and benedictions. Small pleas and big intercessions. Conversations with God range from groans without words to multi-page prayers of global significance. And reading the words that others have prayed encourages a fuller prayer life or simply gives us words to pray when we can't find the right ones ourselves.

Timeless Blessings is a collection of prayers that can be used any time you are looking for words to express yourself to God—in your daily quiet time or for momentous occasions. There are prayers to share with family or friends and toasts for special events. Additionally, the history that accompanies each prayer adds a layer of meaning and significance.

Our hope as you use this book is that you connect personally and uniquely with God; that you will take the time to share what is on your heart with Him—whether that comes from these prayers or your own thoughts. But most of all, we pray that you will earnestly listen to His response as He transforms your heart prayer by prayer.

The Lord's Prayer

Our Father in heaven,
Hallowed be Your name.
Your kingdom come.
Your will be done
On earth as it is in heaven.
Give us this day our daily bread.
And forgive us our debts,
As we forgive our debtors.
And do not lead us into temptation,
But deliver us from the evil one.
For Yours is the kingdom and the power and the glory
forever. Amen.

MATTHEW 6:9-13 NKJV

In the book of Luke, Jesus's disciples ask Him to teach them how to pray. Jesus's response, recorded in Matthew 6 and in Luke 11, is referred to as *the Lord's Prayer* or the *Our Father*.

Recited around the globe throughout the centuries, from sailors on the sea to children in the classroom, it has united believers under one Father.

A musical setting of the Lord's Prayer was written by Albert Hay Malotte in 1935 and recorded by numerous singers, including Perry Como, Doris Day, Gracie Fields, Andrea Bocelli, Mario Lanza, Elvis Presley, Ronnie Milsap, Sergio Franchi (performed on the Ed Sullivan Show), Barbra Streisand, Kristin Chenoweth, The Statler Brothers, Aretha Franklin, The Beach Boys, and LeAnn Rimes. The song's melody is very similar to that of Schubert's "Ave Maria."

Early Prayer from a Friend of the Disciples

We ask Thee, O Lord, to be our supporter and our helper.
To those of us who are afflicted, free us...
raise the fallen, show Thyself to the needy,
heal the sick, convert Thy wayward people,
feed the hungry, deliver our captives,
support the weak, encourage the faint-hearted.
Let all nations know that Thou alone are God
and Jesus Christ is Thy Son,
and we are Thy people, the sheep of Thy flock.

CLEMENT OF ROME (CIRCA AD 96)

Clement of Rome is one of just a handful of acknowledged leaders of the first-century church. Believed to be one of the first bishops of Rome, consecrated by the apostle Peter himself, Clement is known for writing the First Epistle of Clement, which is a letter addressed to the church at Corinth. His epistle may be the earliest existing Christian document outside the New Testament books, believed by scholars to be written at the same time as Revelation.

Prayer of Trust in
God's Heavenly Promise

My God, let me know and love Thee,
so that I may find my happiness in Thee.
Since I cannot fully achieve this on earth,
help me to improve daily until I may do so to the full.
Enable me to know Thee ever more on earth,
so that I may know Thee perfectly in heaven.
Enable me to love Thee ever more on earth,
so that I may love Thee perfectly in heaven.
In that way my joy may be great on earth,
and perfect with Thee in heaven.
O God of truth, grant me the happiness of heaven
so that my joy may be full in accord with Thy promise....
Let my mind dwell on that happiness,
my tongue speak of it, my heart pine for it,
my mouth pronounce it, my soul hunger for it,
my flesh thirst for it, and my entire being desire it
until I enter through death in the joy of my Lord forever.
Amen.

Augustine of Hippo (354–430)

Augustine of Hippo was an early Christian theologian from Algeria who explored different philosophical beliefs before converting to Christianity at thirty-one years old. His interest in philosophical questions started when he was nineteen and continued through his life. Viewed by some as a link between the ancient and medieval worlds, Augustine was also interested in the practical concerns of the church of his time. His writings, such as *City of God* and *Confessions*, were influential in Western Christianity and philosophy and are still read today.

The Prayer of Saint Francis

Lord, make me an instrument of Thy peace.

Where there is hatred, let me sow love,

Where there is injury, let me sow pardon,

Where there is doubt, faith,

Where there is despair, hope,

Where there is darkness, light,

And where there is sadness, joy.

O Divine Master,

Grant that I may not seek so much

to be consoled as to console,

To be understood as to understand,

To be loved as to love.

For it is in giving that we receive,

It is in forgiving that we are forgiven,

And it is in dying that we are born to eternal life.

While widely attributed to St. Francis of Assisi, who lived in the second century BC, the prayer is now recognized as first appearing in print in a small magazine in France in 1912. Still referred to as The Prayer of Saint Francis, this gentle yearning for the guiding hand of a loving God has been quoted widely, especially in the last forty years: in movies and television shows, by politicians, in royal weddings, and as part of murals on buildings. The song, often referred to as "Make Me a Channel of Your Peace," was brought to a new audience when *Britain's Got Talent* singing sensation Susan Boyle included it on her best-selling album *The Gift*, her first Christmas album.

Aaron's Benediction

*The L*ord *bless you and keep you;*
*The L*ord *make His face shine upon you,*
And be gracious to you;
*The L*ord *lift up His countenance upon you,*
And give you peace.

Numbers 6:24-26 nkjv

The ancient practice of the spoken blessing was first mentioned in Genesis 14 when the mysterious Melchizedek, priest of God Most High and king of Salem, appears to Abraham. It continued through the life of Abraham's grandson Jacob: he deceives his brother in order to receive his father's blessing (Genesis 27), he demands a blessing after a pre-dawn wrestling match with God (Genesis 32), and he blesses his children, as his own father did, in the last days of his life (Genesis 49).

As part of God's chosen line of priests, Aaron and his sons were given a word-for-word blessing that they were to proclaim over the assembly. "So they will put my name on the Israelites, and I will bless them" (Numbers 6:27 NKJV). They were forever blessed to be called by the name of God.

Today, synagogues still utilize this blessing as a benediction. With arms outstretched, thumbs touching, the four fingers on each hand split into two sets of two fingers each (thus forming the Hebrew letter Shin, and emblem for Shaddai), rabbis say a blessing over the congregants.

The traditional hand positioning has boldly gone where no one has gone before by becoming the inspiration for the Vulcan hand salute, which Jewish actor Lenard Nimoy created for his character on the television show *Star Trek*.

A Prayer to Our Lord and Master

Lord and Master of my life,
Keep from me the spirit of indifference and discouragement,
Lust of power and idle chatter.
Instead, grant me, Your servant,
The spirit of wholeness of being,
humble-mindedness, patience, and love.
O Lord and King,
Grant me the grace to be aware of my sins
And not to judge my brother;
For You are blessed now and ever and forever.
Amen.

ATTRIBUTED TO ST. EPHREM THE SYRIAN (306-373)

St. Ephrem, a deacon and a theologian of the fourth century, was a prolific writer who created hymns, poems, sermons, and commentaries, many of which were for encouragement of the church during troubled times. He lived during and after the reign of Constantine, the Roman emperor who put an end to penalties, including death, for professing Christians. Constantine himself converted to Christianity and created tolerance for other religions. After the emperor's death, foreign armies saw opportunity and attacked. St. Ephrem would shepherd his church through the turmoil of war as well as against the many heretical sects that threatened to divide the Early Church. He died from the plague after catching it from those to whom he had been ministering.

The specific requests and petitions of this prayer from St. Ephrem make it just as viable today as it was to the people of his time.

Lifted in God's Arms

Holy God, You have shown me light and life.
You are stronger than any natural power.
Accept the words from my heart
That struggle to reach You.
Accept the silent thoughts and feelings
That are offered to You.
Clear my mind of the clutter of useless facts.
Bend down to me, and lift me in Your arms.
Make me holy as You are holy.
Give me a voice to sing of Your love to others.

This prayer is from an early papyrus document, dated between the second and fourth centuries. In the second century, the Church was just starting to stand on its own without the influence of the eyewitnesses of Jesus. The term Christianity was first recorded in AD 107, and the Church was already defending the truth of Christianity against other doctrines.

These ancient words show the unknown writer's love for a personal God, even to the request that, like a child with a loving father, the writer be lifted into God's arms.

One Day in Your Courts

Hear my prayer, LORD God Almighty....
Better is one day in your courts
than a thousand elsewhere;
I would rather be a doorkeeper in the house of my God
than dwell in the tents of the wicked.
For the LORD God is a sun and shield;
the LORD bestows favor and honor;
no good thing does he withhold
from those whose walk is blameless.
LORD Almighty, blessed is the one who trusts in you.

PSALM 84:8, 10-12 NIV

Psalm 84 has recently become popular through a beloved worship song written by Matt Redman in 2000. Not only is it sung in churches nationwide, it has also been recorded by other contemporary singers such as Chris Tomlin and the group Kutless.

The words unite listeners with the author (identified in the Bible as simply "one of the sons of Korah"), expressing a deep desire to be near the Almighty—who protects us, honors us, and withholds nothing good from us when we walk with Him.

Prayer of Devotion

Thanks be to Thee, my Lord Jesus Christ
For all the benefits Thou hast given me,
For all the pains and insults Thou hast borne for me.
O most merciful Redeemer, friend and brother,
May I know Thee more clearly,
Love Thee more dearly,
Follow Thee more nearly.

RICHARD OF CHICHESTER (1197-1253)

Richard of Chichester was an orphan of an upper-class family in England. Once he became of age, he refused a portion of the inheritance of his parents' estate in order to pursue a life of study and the church. He became the chancellor at Oxford, then left to study theology and eventually became the bishop at Chichester.

During the elections for bishop, King Henry III preferred another candidate and a conflict ensued. An appeal to the pope was made and Richard was confirmed. Still, the king withheld the properties of the bishop for two years until threatened with excommunication. In the meantime, Richard lived in a parish priest's house, visiting members of his congregation on foot. He was known to be thrifty and observed a vegetarian diet as well as a rigid temperance.

Today, Richard is remembered largely for this prayer, skillfully translated from Latin in 1898 with a rhyming triplet, which he reportedly recited on his deathbed.

Prayer before Study

Ineffable Creator....
Pour forth a ray of Your brightness
into the darkened places of my mind....
Refine my speech and pour forth upon my lips
the goodness of Your blessing.
Grant to me keenness of mind,
capacity to remember, skill in learning,
subtlety to interpret, and eloquence in speech.
May You guide the beginning of my work,
direct its progress, and bring it to completion.
You who are true God and true Man,
Who live and reign, world without end.
Amen.

THOMAS AQUINAS (1225-1274)

Thomas Aquinas's influence is evident with almost every theological issue in Western theology today. He was a Dominican friar and priest from Italy who believed that people need help from God to understand any and all truth, and he criticized philosophers for missing the true wisdom found in Christian revelation.

During Thomas's years of schooling he was particularly drawn to more contemporary monastic orders, ones that emphasized a life of spiritual service rather than the traditional sheltered life of study. His family objected to these new principles to the point of kidnapping him for a year, attempting to "deprogram" his new beliefs. Despite that, when released, he went back to the Dominican order and was ordained in 1250. Later, while studying for his doctorate, his modesty was misperceived and his classmates thought him dim-witted. However, after reading Thomas's thesis, his professor proclaimed, "We call this young man a dumb ox, but his bellowing in doctrine will one day resound throughout the world!" When his education was complete, Thomas was sought after for his wisdom at many universities and institutions.

Prayer of Awe

O eternal Trinity,
You are a deep sea in which the more
I seek the more I find, and the more I find,
the more I seek to know You.
You fill us insatiably, because the soul,
before the abyss which You are, is always famished;
and hungering for You, O eternal Trinity,
it desires to behold truth in Your light.
As the thirsty hart pants after
the fount of living water,
so does my soul long to...see You as You are, in truth.

CATHERINE OF SIENA (1347-1380)

Catherine of Siena was a famous medieval theologian. At the age of seven she consecrated herself to Christ. Throughout her life she tended the poor, the very sick, and the destitute, and gave her time to help convert the lost. Catherine was known for having a happy countenance even in dire circumstances or during persecution from fellow contemporaries. Throughout her life she experienced visions; one vision led her to leave her secluded life and enter the political arena where she was a leader in the push for reform in the Church of her time.

Prayer of Surrender

Lord, You know what is best; let this be done or that be done as You please. Give what You will, as much as You will, when You will. Do with me as You know best, as will most please You, and will be for Your greater honor. Place me where You will and deal with me freely in all things. I am in Your hand; turn me about whichever way You will. Behold, I am Your servant, ready to obey in all things. Not for myself do I desire to live, but for You— would that I could do this worthily and perfectly!

THOMAS À KEMPIS (1380-1471)

Thomas à Kempis was a priest, monk, and writer from Germany. Kempis copied two Bibles (each ten volumes) and wrote sermons, letters, and biographies of the saints. His most famous book, *The Imitation of Christ*, is a devotional that was eventually translated into over fifty languages. After the Bible, it became the most widely translated book in Christian literature, bringing clarity and comfort to millions during a spiritually disillusioning time of rampant corruption in the Church.

To illustrate this point, the publisher of the first edition of *The Imitation of Christ* received a commendation from George Pinkhamer, a respected theologian in the 1400s, stating, "Nothing more holy, nothing more honorable, nothing more religious, nothing in fine more profitable for the Christian commonweal can you ever do than to make known these works of Thomas à Kempis."

The Right Words

Lord, give me grace to hold righteousness in all things
That I may lead a clean and blessed life...and that I may
understand the treacherous and deceitful
falseness of the devil.
Make me mild, peaceable, courteous, and temperate.
And make me steadfast and strong.
Also, Lord, give Thou to me that I be quiet in words
And that I speak what is appropriate.
Amen.

JOHN WYCLIFFE (C. 1328-1384)

John Wycliffe, a theologian, pastor, and instructor at Oxford, lived in England during the 1300s. He is well known for opposing the injustices of his day, including the corruption in the Church. His passion for promoting the authority of the Bible was the driving principle of the Reformation, which would take place two centuries later. He preached that laypeople could understand the Word of God themselves if they could read it in their native tongue. Wycliffe was the first to translate the Bible from Latin into English.

Wycliffe Bible Translators was formed in the 1940s with the goal that everyone should be able to read God's Word in their own language. Named after John Wycliffe, the organization has completed more than seven hundred translations.

A Sailor's Early Morning Prayer

Blessed be the light of day
And the Holy Cross, we say;
And the Lord of Veritie*
And the Holy Trinity.
Blessed be th' immortal soul
And the Lord who keeps it whole,
Blessed be the light of day
And He who sends the night away.

*Veritie: something that is true, or divine truth

Five hundred years ago, before maritime inventions helped seafarers navigate across the wide expansive oceans, sailors were quite religious. They saw God as in control of all nature, as recorded in Psalm 107: "He stilled the storm to a whisper; the waves of the sea were hushed.... He guided them to their desired haven."

This short prayer was typical of what a sailor would sing out at the break of day while at sea.

The Shepherd's Psalm

The LORD is my shepherd,
I shall not want.
He makes me lie down in green pastures;
He leads me beside quiet waters.
He restores my soul;
He guides me in the paths of righteousness
For His name's sake.
Even though I walk through
the valley of the shadow of death,
I fear no evil, for You are with me;
Your rod and Your staff, they comfort me.
You prepare a table before me
in the presence of my enemies;
You have anointed my head with oil;
My cup overflows.
Surely goodness and lovingkindness will follow me
all the days of my life,
And I will dwell in the house of the LORD forever.

PSALM 23:1-6 NASB

Written by David, a shepherd boy chosen by God to be king because of his passionate heart. (1 Samuel 16:7-12), Psalm 23 gives us a clear picture of that heart—of his trust in a tender, nurturing God to gently care for his daily needs and generously guide his future.

This beautiful chapter is likely the most recognized and oft-quoted passage in Scripture. It was quoted by 911 hero Todd Beamer aboard United Airlines Flight 93, and was also recited by George W. Bush in his Address to the Nation to comfort a country in mourning that day.

This tribute to the Lord our Shepherd, written thousands of years before the birth of Jesus, continues to comfort through promises of Christ's nearness and care.

Mealtime Blessing

O heavenly Father, who is the fountain of full treasure of all goodness, we call upon You to show Your mercies upon us, Your children, and bless these gifts which we receive by Your compassionate generosity, granting us grace to use them sensibly and purely, according to Your blessed will; so that as a result we may acknowledge You to be the author and giver of all good things; and, above all, that we may remember to continually seek the spiritual food of Your Word, by which our souls may be nourished.

JOHN KNOX (C. 1513-1572)

John Knox was a clergyman from Scotland and a leader of the Protestant Reformation. He is known as a fearless revolutionary who taught that it was the Christian's duty to oppose unjust government to bring about moral and spiritual change. He is known as the founder of the Presbyterian denomination.

Prayer for Clear Vision

Lord, give us weak eyes for things, which are of no account, and clear eyes for all Your truth.

SOREN KIERKEGAARD (1813-1855)

Kierkegaard was a Danish philosopher, theologian, and prolific author in the golden age of intellectual and artistic expression. His writings included not only philosophy and theology but also literary criticism, devotional literature, and fiction. He is known as the "Father of Existentialism," but his literary experimentation and his enlightening representation of biblical characters to bring out relevance are today valued above his many other contributions.

He believed that each individual is responsible for giving meaning to life and living with passion.

Farewell Prayer

At last, my Beloved, we are going to see each other.
It is time for us to be on the way.

TERESA OF AVILA (1575-1582), ON HER DEATHBED

Teresa of Avila was a Carmelite nun from Avila, Spain, whose paternal grandfather was a Jewish convert to Christianity. Teresa's mother gave her early instruction in Christianity, but died when she was fourteen. When Teresa became overly attached to boys, clothes, and her appearance in her teens, her father decided to send her to a convent when she was sixteen. She eventually grew to enjoy life at the convent and chose to remain a nun rather than be married.

She struggled with divided devotion, and then illness, until early in her forties when a priest helped her turn her heart to God in prayer and her love of God grew. She said, "The memory of the favor God has granted does more to bring such a person back to God than all the infernal punishments imaginable."

She was an influence in a period of Catholic revival, and a proponent of contemplative life through mental prayer. She described contemplative (mental) prayer is a close sharing between friends, with Him who loves us.

An Evening Prayer

*O Lord God, who has given [mankind] the night for rest,
as Thou hast created the day in which he may employ
himself in labor, grant, I pray, that my body may so
rest during this night that my mind cease not to be
awake to Thee, nor my heart faint or be overcome with
[weariness], preventing it from adhering steadfastly to
the love of Thee. While laying aside my cares to relax
and relieve my mind, may I not, in the meanwhile, forget
Thee, nor may the remembrance of Thy goodness and
grace, which ought always to be deeply engraven
on my mind, escape my memory.*

JOHN CALVIN (1509-1564)

John Calvin was a French theologian who was one of the leaders during the Protestant Reformation. He broke away from the Catholic church in 1530. His beliefs led to Calvinism, which stressed the sovereignty of God in all things, in salvation and all of life.

Praise for Victory
Over the Impossible

*Praise be to our eternal God, our Lord, who gives to all
those who walk in His ways victory over all things which
seem impossible.... Our Redeemer has granted this victory.*

Christopher Columbus (1451-1506)

Christopher Columbus's return to Spain after discovering the New World could have looked very different. His mission had been a success. He'd proven the wisest, the most reputable, wrong. Yet, instead of sailing back into port on the good ship *I Told You So*, he wrote to his royal financiers, Queen Isabella and King Ferdinand, while anchored off the Canary Islands near Africa. He gave them detailed accounts of his travels, then ended his letter by giving glory to whom it was due. The Redeemer had "granted the victory to our illustrious King and Queen and their kingdoms, which have acquired great fame by an event of such high importance, in which all Christendom ought to rejoice, and which it ought to celebrate with great festivals and the offering of solemn thanks to the Holy Trinity with many sincere prayers...." No personal pronoun in sight.

Travel Blessing

May the road rise up to meet you,
May the wind be always at your back.
May the sun shine warm upon your face;
The rains fall soft upon your fields, and until we meet again,
May God hold you in the palm of His hand.

TRADITIONAL GAELIC BLESSING

Thought to have been composed between the fourth and seventh centuries AD, this Celtic prayer is just one example of early Christian blessings. Communities in Ireland worked together to produce beautiful art, crafts, and music. Their prayer life reflected the connection they had to nature and their devotion to God. The result was some of the most inspirational and beautiful church literature in history. And this prayer specifically has become a popular parting or travel blessing.

The Geneva Bible Blessing

I pray that your love may abound yet more and more in knowledge, and in all judgment, that ye may allow those things which are best, that ye may be pure, and without offense, until the day of Christ.

PHILIPPIANS 1:9-10 GNV

The Geneva Bible (the passage on page 48 is from the 1599 edition) was significant—it was the first Bible to use chapters and numbered verses. It came with study material written by Reformation leaders John Calvin, John Knox, and others, to help explain and interpret the Scriptures for the average reader. This prayer from Paul for the Philippians was likely on the hearts of those early Christian leaders as they labored to put the living Word in the hands and on the nightstands of their family, friends, and community for the first time in history.

Early Family Devotions

Blessed is the one
who does not walk in step with the wicked
or stand in the way that sinners take
or sit in the company of mockers,
but whose delight is in the law of the LORD,
and who meditates on his law day and night.
That person is like a tree planted by streams of water,
which yields its fruit in season
and whose leaf does not wither—
whatever they do prospers.
Not so the wicked!
They are like chaff that the wind blows away.
Therefore the wicked will not stand in the judgment,
nor sinners in the assembly of the righteous.
For the LORD watches over the way of the righteous,
but the way of the wicked leads to destruction.

PSALM 1:1-6 NIV

The opening psalm describes the benefits of delighting in the law of the Lord. Early Jewish families used this unattributed psalm in family worship. It was memorized by the children, quoted, and sung repeatedly.

Timeless Arrow Prayers*

*O Lord, never suffer us to think that we can
stand by ourselves, and not need Thee.*

JOHN DONNE (1573-1631), AN ENGLISH POET, SATIRIST, LAWYER
AND CLERIC IN THE CHURCH OF ENGLAND

*O Lord, may I be directed what to do
and what to leave undone.*

ELIZABETH FRY (1780-1845), AN ENGLISH QUAKER WELL-KNOWN FOR
HER DRIVE FOR MORE HUMANE TREATMENT OF PRISONERS

*May Your grace, O Lord, make that possible to me
which seems impossible to me by nature.*

AMY CARMICHAEL (1867-1951), A MISSIONARY IN INDIA FOR FIFTY-FIVE
YEARS WHO DESCRIBED MISSIONARY WORK SIMPLY AS "A CHANCE TO DIE"

Father, forgive them, they know not what they do.

CHRIST, OUR PASSOVER, WHEN SACRIFICED FOR US.

* Arrow Prayers are best described as short, to-the-point phrases that one shoots up
to heaven to entreat God for His help, ask for His forgiveness, or praise Him for that
specific moment.

Prayer for Purity

Create in me a clean heart, O God,
And renew a steadfast spirit within me.
Do not cast me away from Your presence,
And do not take Your Holy Spirit from me.
Restore to me the joy of Your salvation,
And uphold me by Your generous Spirit.

PSALM 51:10-12 NKJV

This prayer for purity is often quoted in inaugural prayers for corporate repentance. "Create in Me a Clean Heart" has been set to music by many artists, including Keith Green, a Contemporary Christian artist in the late seventies and early eighties who shocked many in the industry when, at the height of his career, he refused to charge for his albums and concerts.

From the *Book of Common Prayer*

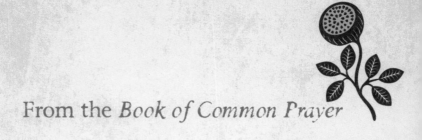

Holy, holy, holy, Lord God of hosts,
Heaven and earth are full of thy glory:
Glory be to thee, O Lord most high.

BOOK OF COMMON PRAYER, 1662

Almighty and eternal God, so draw our hearts to Thee,
so guide our minds, so fill our imaginations, so control
our wills, that we may be wholly Thine, utterly dedicated
unto Thee; and then use us, we pray Thee, as Thou wilt,
and always to Thy glory and the welfare of Thy people;
through our Lord and Savior Jesus Christ.
Amen.

BOOK OF COMMON PRAYER, 1979,
PROTESTANT EPISCOPAL CHURCH IN THE USA

First published in 1549, the *Book of Common Prayer* included the words of structured church services. It was ground breaking as the first prayer book to include the complete service for daily and Sunday worship in English. It also included morning prayers and evening prayers, with the Old Testament and New Testament readings by day.

The *Book of Common Prayer* is considered a major work of English literature. It has had a great religious and literary influence since its introduction in the mid-1500s.

The Apostles' Creed

I believe in God, the Father Almighty,
maker of heaven and earth.
And in Jesus Christ, his only Son, our Lord,
who was conceived by the Holy Spirit,
born of the virgin Mary,
suffered under Pontius Pilate,
was crucified, died, and was buried.
He descended into hell.
On the third day He rose again from the dead.
He ascended into heaven
and sits at the right hand of God the Father Almighty.
From thence He will come to judge the living and the dead.
I believe in the Holy Spirit, the holy Christian Church,
the communion of saints, the forgiveness of sins,
the resurrection of the body, and the life everlasting.
Amen.

The Apostles' Creed is an early statement of Christian belief. The words "Apostles' Creed" first appeared in history in a letter dated 390 from a synod in Italy. Although not directly written by the apostles, the creed reflects and solidified the theology of the church in its first century of existence. It is used by a number of Christian denominations today, including Catholic, Lutheran, Anglican, Western Orthodoxy, Presbyterians, Methodists, and Congregationalists.

Traditional Catholic
Mealtime Prayer

Bless us, O Lord, and these Thy gifts, which we are about to receive, from Thy bounty, through Christ, our Lord. Amen.

There is no strict rule about the wording of mealtime prayers, but this short blessing from the Catholic catechism is one recited around many tables. The prayer before meals is known as a "blessing," for it consists in the invoking of God's blessing upon us and upon what we are about to receive. It is also known as "grace," from the Latin word *gratiae*, meaning "thanks."

Norwegian Mealtime Blessing

In Jesus's name we go to the table
To eat and drink by Thy word;
In God's honor and for our benefit
We receive the food in Jesus's name.

Many generational family prayers are passed down in the words of the country from which they came. Mealtime family blessings, like this one translated from Norwegian, came across the Atlantic in the 1800s. Kitchens in the new country were christened with prayers from the old, helping keep cultural ties to their Provider intact when surrounded by neighbors whose kitchen-table prayers sounded very different. These prayers were often preserved in family Bibles or in framed needlepoint long after the loved ones who taught the prayers were gone.

"My Winter's Past" Prayer Poem

As spring the winter does succeed,
And leaves the naked trees do dress,
The earth all black is clothed in green;
At sunshine each their joy express.
My sun's returned with healing wings.
My soul and body do rejoice;
My heart exults and praises sing
To You who heard my wailing voice.
My winter's past, my storms are gone,
And former clouds now seem all fled;
But, if they must eclipse again,
I'll run where I was amply fed.
I have a shelter from the storm,
A shadow from the fainting heat;
I have access unto Your throne
You who are God so wondrous great.

ANNE BRADSTREET (1612-1672)

Raised in England, Anne Bradstreet moved to the colonies as a married woman of eighteen in 1630. Her love and fascination with her new home was evident in her poetry. She was the first woman poet to publish in the colonies. Her collection of poetry titled *The Tenth Muse Lately Sprung Up in America* was taken to England by her brother and published in 1650.

This prayer is from *Religious Experiences and Occasional Pieces,* which was left to her children and published after her death. She proclaimed that it was a record of God dealing with her from childhood through her last days. Although her poetry was not well known during her lifetime, it won critical acclaim in the twentieth century and continues to be well respected in literary circles, especially her later work, which is deeply personal.

Praise for Creation

All things bright and beautiful,
All creatures great and small,
All things wise and wonderful,
The Lord God made them all.

He gave us eyes to see them,
And lips that we may tell
How great is God Almighty,
Who has made all things well.

Mrs. C.F. Alexander (1818-1895)

Mrs. Cecil Francis Alexander was a hymn writer and poet from Dublin, England. This hymn first appeared in 1848 in her book *Hymns for Little Children*. Alexander may have found inspiration for her hymn from a line in *The Rime of the Ancient Mariner*, written in the late 1700s by Samuel Taylor Coleridge: "He prayeth best, who loveth best;/ All things great and small;/ For the dear God who loveth us,/ He made and loveth all."

English author James Herriot used three lines from this hymn for three best-selling semi-autobiographical books he wrote about a veterinary practice in northern England, which was later adapted for television and film.

Thanksgiving and Praise

O God our Father,
We would thank Thee for all the bright things of life.
Help us to see them, and to count them, and to
Remember them, that our lives may flow
in ceaseless praise;
For the sake of Jesus Christ our Lord.

JOHN HENRY JOWETT (1846-1923)

The Rev. Dr. John Henry Jowett, renowned English preacher and writer, was pastor of the Fifth Avenue Presbyterian Church in New York City from 1911 to 1918. Though he did not have the dramatic flair of some that shared the pulpit during his era, the knowledge and clarity that went into the sermons he prepared and read, coupled with the way he lived his life, drew great respect and large audiences. Under his leadership, the congregation more than doubled in size and as many as one thousand would-be worshippers had to be turned away for lack of room on Sunday mornings.

The Shema: A Daily Declaration of Faith

Hear, O Israel: the Lord our God, the Lord is one. Love the Lord your God with all your heart and with all your soul and with all your strength. These commandments that I give you today are to be on your hearts. Impress them on your children. Talk about them when you sit at home and when you walk along the road, when you lie down and when you get up. Tie them as symbols on your hands and bind them on your foreheads. Write them on the doorframes of your houses and on your gates.

Deuteronomy 6:4-9 niv

This section of Scripture in Deuteronomy is referred to as the Shema in Jewish culture, where it is the centerpiece in morning and evening prayers. This declaration of faith is recited aloud with one's right hand over the eyes to eliminate distraction.

The Shema consists first of three sections that link together as one prayer. The first section is given on page 68. The second is found in Deuteronomy 11:13–21 and speaks of the benefits of obedience and the consequences that come through disobedience. The third section is found in Numbers 15:37–41, in which God instructs the Israelites to wear tassels to help them remember and obey His commandments.

Come, Thou Long Expected Jesus

Come, thou long expected Jesus,
born to set Thy people free;
from our fears and sins release us,
let us find our rest in Thee.
Israel's strength and consolation,
hope of all the earth Thou art;
dear desire of every nation,
joy of every longing heart.

CHARLES WESLEY (1707-1788)

On January 1, 1739, Charles Wesley's brother John gathered a group of friends for a prayer vigil. The all-night intercession was a precursor to events that would change the course of history for both Brits and Americans. In a famous journal entry, John wrote, "About three in the morning as we were continuing instant in prayer the power of God came mightily upon us insomuch that many cried out for exceeding joy and many fell to the ground."

This encounter in the early hours of the morning propelled John Wesley out of the prayer room into a world-changing ministry. Joining his brother Charles, who would become well known for composing some of the greatest hymns of all time, and a young revolutionary preacher by the name of George Whitefield, the three men made an impact like no other on Europe and North America that has lasted for generations.

Mary's Song

My soul glorifies the Lord and my spirit
rejoices in God my Savior,
for he has been mindful of the humble state of his servant.
From now on all generations will call me blessed,
for the Mighty One has done great things for me—
holy is his name.
His mercy extends to those who fear him,
from generation to generation.
He has performed mighty deeds with his arm;
he has scattered those who are proud
in their inmost thoughts.
He has brought down rulers from their thrones
but has lifted up the humble.
He has filled the hungry with good things
but has sent the rich away empty.
He has helped his servant Israel, remembering to be merciful
to Abraham and his descendants forever,
just as he promised our ancestors.

LUKE 1:46-55 NIV

This song erupts from the lips of Mary after a divine connection occurs between two unborn babies. When Mary arrived to visit her relative Elizabeth and called a greeting, the baby in Elizabeth leaped and she was filled with the Holy Spirit. This resulted in Elizabeth's loud three-part blessing to Mary: "Blessed are you among women, and blessed is the child you will bear!... Blessed is she who has believed that the Lord would fulfill his promises to her!" (Luke 1:42-45). Mary's response, also known as the Magnificat (from the first word of the Latin version), is sung or spoken in church services of various denominations internationally.

A Child's Bedtime Prayer

Now I lay me down to sleep,
I pray the Lord my soul to keep;
If I should die before I wake,
I pray the Lord my soul to take;
For Jesus's sake.
Amen.

<small>As repeated by John Quincy Adams</small>

As a young boy, John Quincy Adams heard the sounds of the Revolutionary War from a hill near his home. It instilled in him a lifelong devotion to freedom. His interest in a political career budded a short time later when his father was sent to Europe as a commissioner to negotiate peace with Great Britain and took ten-year-old John with him.

John's love for his newly founded country and his vision for freedom held strong through almost seventy years of public service, including his years as president. He was one of the most influential men in building a strong foundation for the United States.

"Now I Lay Me Down to Sleep," a child's prayer that can be traced to the early 1700s, was prayed by John Quincy Adams nightly for many years. He also prayed the Lord's Prayer but had a special affinity for this one because it suited him, he said. A simple prayer, it likely soothed the soul of a man dealing with complications on a daily basis.

Close of Day Prayer

Father of Heaven! whose goodness has brought us in safety to the close of this day, dispose our hearts in fervent prayer. Another day is now gone, and added to those, for which we were before accountable. Teach us, Almighty Father, to consider this solemn truth, as we should do, that we may feel the importance of every day, and every hour as it passes, and earnestly strive to make a better use of what Thy goodness may yet bestow on us, than we have done of the time past.

JANE AUSTEN (1775-1817)

Well-known English author Jane Austen came from a religious family: her father, two brothers, and four cousins were clergymen. The profession is well represented in her novels and letters, although these prayers, from her personal correspondence, are often overlooked by biographers.

This prayer is excerpted from one of three that survive on two sheets of paper, with "Prayers Composed by my ever dear Sister Jane" hand-written on the outside fold. The prayers were also likely read by Austen or a member of the family, in the common practice of assembling the entire household for evening prayers before bedtime. The form of her prayers is said to echo those in the *Book of Common Prayer* (1662), well-known at that time, which were often recited or repeated together. Although more formal sounding than prayers today, Jane Austen's prayer reflects a trust in the control and goodness of God, and a desire to make best use of the goodness she was confident He would again bestow.

The Beatitudes

Blessed are the poor in spirit,
for theirs is the kingdom of heaven.
Blessed are those who mourn,
for they will be comforted.
Blessed are the meek,
for they will inherit the earth.
Blessed are those who hunger and thirst for righteousness,
for they will be filled.
Blessed are the merciful,
for they will be shown mercy.
Blessed are the pure in heart,
for they will see God.
Blessed are the peacemakers,
for they will be called children of God.
Blessed are those who are persecuted because of
righteousness,
for theirs is the kingdom of heaven.

*Blessed are you when people insult you,
persecute you and falsely say all kinds of evil
against you because of me. Rejoice and be
glad, because great is your reward in heaven,
for in the same way they persecuted the
prophets who were before you.*

MATTHEW 5:3-12 NIV

This passage, referred to as the Beatitudes, is the opening
to Jesus's famous Sermon on the Mount. "Beatitude" comes
from the Latin word *beatitudo*, meaning "blessedness."
When Jesus said "blessed are" in each of the beatitudes, He
was saying "divinely happy and fortunate are" those whom
He described. Jesus takes our ideas about commonsense
happiness and sets it on its ear. The value system of the day—
and also of today—has been changed to a Kingdom priority.

The Church of the Beatitudes in Israel is located near the site
where Jesus preached the Sermon on the Mount.

Prayer for the Heart of a Nation

Almighty God; we make our earnest prayer that Thou wilt keep the United States in Thy holy protection; and Thou wilt incline the hearts of the citizens to cultivate a spirit of subordination and obedience to government; and entertain a brotherly affection and love for one another and for their fellow citizens of the United States at large.

And finally that Thou wilt most graciously be pleased to dispose us all to do justice, to love mercy, and to demean ourselves with that charity, humility, and pacific temper of mind which were the characteristics of the Divine Author of our blessed religion, and without a humble imitation of whose example in these things we can never hope to be a happy nation. Grant our supplication, we beseech Thee, through Jesus Christ our Lord. Amen.

GEORGE WASHINGTON (1732-1799), WRITTEN TO THE GOVERNORS AND STATES OF THE NEW NATION ON JUNE 8, 1783

These words of George Washington are found in two churches: on a plaque on the wall of St. Paul's Chapel in New York City, and at Pohick Church in Fairfax County, Virginia, where Washington served as vestryman.

John F. Kennedy cited this prayer from Washington in his address to the International Christian Leadership, Inc., in 1961. Every president has taken courage, Kennedy said, when told that the Lord "will be with thee. He will not fail thee nor forsake thee. Fear not—neither be thou dismayed."

German Mealtime Blessing

Come, Lord Jesus, be our guest,
And let Thy gifts to us be blessed.
Amen.

ATTRIBUTED TO MARTIN LUTHER (1483-1586)

Anglican (Church of England) Mealtime Prayer

Dear Lord, thank You for this food.
Bless the hands that prepared it.
Bless it to our use and us to Your service,
and make us ever mindful of the needs of others.
Through Christ our Lord we pray. Amen.

Prayer of Thanksgiving

Thankfulness, in character,
O Lord, that lends me life
Lend me a heart replete with thankfulness!

HENRY VI, PART 2 BY WILLIAM SHAKESPEARE (1564-1616)

Peaceful Sleep

In peace I will lie down and sleep,
for you alone, LORD,
make me dwell in safety.

PSALM 4:8 NIV

Under His Watch and Wing

Keep me as the apple of Your eye;
Hide me under the shadow of Your wings.

PSALM 17:8 NKJV

Jesus Prays for Us

*Father.... This is eternal life: that they know you, the
only true God, and Jesus Christ, whom you have sent.
I have brought you glory on earth by finishing the
work you gave me to do....
My prayer is not that you take them out of the world
but that you protect them from the evil one....
Sanctify them by the truth; your word is truth.*

JOHN 17:1, 3-4, 15, 17 NIV

Revivalist D. L. Moody (1837–1899) believed the Lord's Prayer should more properly be attributed to John 17, as it is the longest recorded prayer of Jesus. The prayers of Jesus were short in public but long in private; Jesus was known to spend the whole night speaking to His Father alone. In this twenty-five-verse prayer, Jesus focuses on His disciples and those who would later believe—whom He mentions no less than fifty times.

Prayer for a Nation

Plead my cause, O L<small>ORD</small>, with those who strive with me;
Fight against those who fight against me.
Take hold of shield and buckler,
And stand up for my help.
Also draw out the spear,
And stop those who pursue me.
Say to my soul, "I am your salvation."

P<small>SALM</small> 35:1-3 NKJV

When it was suggested in 1774 that the first Continental Congress open in prayer, it was almost voted down because the religious diversity in the assembly was thought too great. There were Episcopalians, Quakers, Anabaptists, and Presbyterians who, while united in their love for their country, did not share a worship style or "religious sentiments." Then Samuel Adams weighed in: he would support any gentleman of piety and character who was also a friend to his country. This swayed the collective opinion, and the next morning an Episcopalian clergyman read several prayers and Psalm 35.

John Adams wrote to his wife, Abigail, and described the results of the prayers, reminding her that the previous day they had heard the rumor that Boston had been attacked. "I never saw a greater effect upon an audience. It seemed as if heaven had ordained that psalm to be read on that morning," he wrote. The clergyman then unexpectedly prayed, without the formality of notecards: for America, for Congress, for Massachusetts Bay, and especially for Boston. It filled the hearts of everyone present, Adam reported. He'd never heard a better prayer, and he begged his wife to read Psalm 35.

Prayer for Honest Labor

O God, who hast ordained that
whatever is to be desired should be sought by labor,
and who, by Thy blessing,
bringest honest labor to good effect,
look with mercy upon my studies and endeavors.

Grant me, O Lord, to design only what is lawful and right;
and afford me calmness of mind, and steadiness of purpose,
that I may so do Thy will in this short life
as to obtain happiness in the world to come,
for the sake of Jesus Christ our Lord.
Amen.

SAMUEL JOHNSON (1709-1784)

Samuel Johnson was familiar with labor. A famous English writer, he is considered by many to have been one of the most influential literary figures in history. His literary works include essays, poems, books, and sermons. His most lasting contribution was his famous *Dictionary of the English Language*, which took him nine years to complete and shaped modern English in many ways.

Petition for Vigilance

May He who holds in His hands the destinies of nations, make you worthy of the favors He has bestowed, and enable you, with pure hearts and hands and sleepless vigilance, to guard and defend to the end of time, the great charge He has committed to your keeping.

ANDREW JACKSON (1767-1845)

Although regarded as one of the most controversial presidents in history, Andrew Jackson's aggressive defense of individual liberty resulted in lasting policies.

His relationship with the Holder of Destinies changed significantly in his later years. While Jackson had built a church for his wife, he did not attend with her. When he was seventy, his wife having passed on before him, he approached the elders of the church to join. He was told forgiveness was a condition. While he was willing to forgive his political enemies of late, he was reluctant to forgive the hurt committed against him in his early days serving his country.

Eventually, he forgave. Witnesses of his first attendance as a member saw him on his knees at the altar, tears streaming down his aged cheeks.

He spent the rest of his days showing evidence that he was a true believer: daily reading not only the Bible but also commentaries and a hymnal, as well as saying prayers with his family and servants nightly.

Blessing of Abundance and Beyond

Now to Him who is able to do far more
abundantly beyond all that we ask or think,
according to the power that works within us,
to Him be the glory in the church and in Christ Jesus
to all generations forever and ever. Amen.

EPHESIANS 3:20-21 NASB

Let Thy blessing, O Lord, rest upon our work this day.
Teach us to seek after truth, and enable us to attain it;
but grant that as we increase in the knowledge of earthly
things, we may grow in the knowledge of Thee, whom to
know is life eternal; through Jesus Christ our Lord.

ADAPTED FROM THOMAS ARNOLD (1795-1842),
ENGLISH EDUCATOR AND HISTORIAN

Prayers for Character

O Lord,
give us more charity, more self-denial,
more likeness to Thee.
Teach us to sacrifice our comforts to others,
and our likings for the sake of doing good.
Make us kindly in thought, gentle in word, generous in
deed. Teach us that it is better to give than receive, better
to forget ourselves than to put ourselves forward, better
to minister than to be ministered unto. And to Thee, the
God of love, be all glory and praise, now and forever.

HENRY ALFORD (1810-1871), AN ENGLISH CHURCHMAN, THEOLOGIAN,
SCHOLAR, AND WRITER

Henry Alford, dean of Canterbury, was a churchman with varied accomplishments in theology, general literature, poetry, oratory, painting, and music. He was the fifth successive generation in his family to be a clergyman in the English church. When his mother died in childbirth, he was raised as the only son, and constant companion, of his father. Young Henry wrote his first book at six, titled *Travels of St. Paul*; at nine he wrote a collection of Latin odes and *History of the Jews*; at ten, a series of sermons. It was believed that he could have risen to renown had he focused on one or two areas of interest instead of indefatigably pursuing varied outlets for his great intellect and creativity.

A Prayer to Hold Steady

I'm going to hold steady on You, an' You've got to see me through.

HARRIET TUBMAN (C. 1822-1913)

This arrow prayer was sent up regularly by Harriet Tubman when she led runaway slaves to freedom along the Underground Railroad during the mid-1800s. Called the "Moses" of her people, she escaped the control of abusive masters herself, then returned to the South multiple times to help others—knowing there was a price on her head and her capture would likely mean death.

She recited this prayer as she began each of her escapes. In all her escapes, she did not lose one person. She attributed her success to God.

A Prayer When Words Fail

O Lord! O Lord! Oh, the tears, an' the groans,
an' the moans! O Lord!

Sojourner Truth (c. 1797 – 1893)

Sojourner Truth was one of several children born to parents who were first-generation slaves from Africa. This emotional prayer is one she voiced throughout her long fight against slavery. Though the abuse she experienced and witnessed as a slave gave way to this depth of emotion, she was not overcome with hopelessness. She turned honestly and forcefully to God with her heartache. In 1843, after receiving a vision from God, she changed her name to Sojourner Truth and began traveling and speaking against slavery.

We Two Shall Win

Cowardly, wayward, and weak
I change with the changing sky.
Today so eager and strong
Tomorrow not caring to try.
But He never gives in,
And we two shall win,
Jesus and I.

The Hiding Place tells the story of Corrie ten Boom—growing up in Holland in a dedicated, Christlike family, and their eventual part in the Dutch underground during World War II. It is believed that they were able to save the lives of eight hundred Jews.

This wasn't without cost. After being betrayed by one of their own countryman, Corrie's father, two of her siblings, and one nephew died. Before she died in Ravensbruck prison camp, her sister Betsy said to Corrie that God told her they would both be released before the new year. Shortly after Betsy died, Corrie was allowed to leave due to a "clerical error" in December 1944.

After her release, Corrie ten Boom traveled with the message of forgiveness. She visited sixty countries and wrote many books and devotionals. When given compliments, she pointed to Jesus, often quoting the words of this anonymous poet.

A Healing Touch

O Lord, the hard-won miles
Have worn my stumbling feet:
Oh, soothe me with Thy smiles,
And make my life complete.
The thorns were thick and keen
Where'er I trembling trod;
The way was long between
My wounded feet and God.
Where healing waters flow
Do Thou my footsteps lead.
My heart is aching so;
Thy gracious balm I need.

PAUL LAURENCE DUNBAR (1872-1906)

The son of former slaves, Paul Laurence Dunbar was the first African American to gain widespread fame as a poet. His use of different dialects made his work appeal to a vast audience. This prayer was written not long before he died.

Prayer of Courage for Servicemen

O Lord Jesus Christ, who didst endure unto the end,
and whose courage never failed in the midst of great
dangers: Grant that inspired by Thy example I may
trust completely in Thy promise to be with me even unto
the world's end, and that so, amidst all dangers I may
have a heart inflamed by Thy courage, and a spirit
inspired by Thy faith; through Thy mercy,
O our God, who art blessed, and dost reign,
and govern all things, world without end. Amen.

CAMPAIGN PRAYER BOOK

The *Campaign Prayer Book* was an abridgment of the 1892 *Book of Common Prayer*, made specifically for World War I servicemen. It was one of the first prayer books small enough for soldiers to carry, and contained portions of Scripture and readings used in public worship, as well as prayers and songs. The introduction of the book was written by a former chaplain who recognized the comfort soldiers would feel knowing that the sections of worship services they were reading were the same as those being read by their loved ones so far away at home.

A Prayer for the Church and Government

We praise You and thank You for all of Your gracious election and calling, that You are also the God of the rejected and the uncalled, and that You never cease to deal with each one of us in a fatherly and righteous manner.... We pray for Your church here and in all nations, for the sleeping church, that it may awaken; for the persecuted church, that it may continually rejoice and be assured of what it has in You; and for the confessing church, that it may live not for its own sake, but for Your glory.

We pray for the rulers and the authorities all over the world: for the good ones, that You may preserve them; and for the bad ones, that You may either turn their hearts or put an end to their power, all according to Your will.

Karl Barth (1886–1968)

Referred to as the greatest Protestant theologian of the twentieth century, Karl Barth's influence went beyond the pulpit. Barth held that the God who is revealed in the cross of Jesus overthrows any attempt to ally God with human cultures, achievements, or possessions. He rejected the influence of Nazism on German Christianity, which allowed for the influence of other lords, such as the German *Führer*, Adolf Hitler.

While serving as a theology professor in Germany in the mid-1930s, Karl Barth was fired after refusing to sign an oath of allegiance to Hitler. After the war, he publicly supported both German penitence and reconciliation with churches abroad. Barth's work had a profound impact on twentieth-century theology and figures such as Dietrich Bonhoeffer.

Prayer of Confidence
in Dark Times

O God, early in the morning I cry to You,

Help me to pray, and to think only of You.

I cannot pray alone.

In me there is darkness,

But with You there is light.

I am lonely, but You never leave me.

I am feeble in heart, but You are always strong.

I am restless, but in You there is peace.

In me there is bitterness, but with You patience.

Your ways are beyond my understanding,

But You know the way for me.

<small>DIETRICH BONHOEFFER</small>

Bonhoeffer was a German Lutheran pastor who publicly opposed the Nazi regime. He was one of the founders of the Confessing Church, which maintained that Christ, not the Führer, was the head of the Church.

Activity in the German Resistance movement eventually led to his two-year prison sentence and subsequent hanging. To the end of his life, his prayers, like this one written upon waking up in prison, reflect honest anguish and undeterred trust.

His book *The Cost of Discipleship*, published in 1937, is considered a theological classic.

Answered Prayer in Wartime

*Almighty and most merciful Father, we humbly
beseech Thee, of Thy great goodness, to restrain these
immoderate rains with which we have had to contend.
Grant us fair weather for battle. Graciously hearken to
us as soldiers who call upon Thee that armed with Thy
power, we may advance from victory to victory, and
crush the oppression and wickedness of our enemies,
and establish Thy justice among men and nations.
Amen.*

General George Patton (1885-1945)

During World War II, on December 11 and 12, 1944, General George Patton orchestrated the distribution of prayer cards to every soldier under his command. A quarter of a million copies of the prayer went out, with a specific request for a change in weather. Patton believed the victory would depend on it.

He was a leader who believed in the sovereign control of the Almighty. Prayer, he said, was power. On December 20, the thick ground fog started to break, exposing the enemy. The weather changed so abruptly, it surprised both the Americans and the Nazis. For a few days, the weather suddenly became "perfect for flying" which gave the Allies significant success and the eventual victory.

Blessings for House and Home

I pray heaven to bestow the best of blessing on this house and on all that shall hereafter inhabit it. May none but honest and wise men ever rule under this roof.

John Adams (1735-1826)

Toward the end of World War II, when Franklin Delano Roosevelt was nearing the end of his twelve-year run as president—the longest of any US president in history—he had this quote carved into the stone fireplace in the State Dining Room. He came into office during worldwide economic hardship and left after a worldwide war. His parting request for blessing, wisdom, and honesty for the leaders of his country can still be seen today.

These words came from a letter John Adams wrote to his wife before she joined him at the White House.

A Poem Called "Prayer"

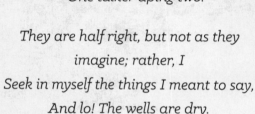

Master, they say that when I seem
To be in speech with You,
Since You make no replies, it's all a dream
—One talker aping two.

They are half right, but not as they
imagine; rather, I
Seek in myself the things I meant to say,
And lo! The wells are dry.

Then, seeing me empty, You forsake
The listener's role, and through
My dead lips breathe and into utterance wake
The thoughts I never knew.

And thus You neither need reply
Nor can; thus while we seem
Two talking, You are One forever, and I
No dreamer, but Your dream.

C. S. Lewis (1898-1963)

C. S. Lewis was one of the most influential writers of his day, and his books continue to inspire and influence leaders and laypeople today. They have sold millions of copies and have been translated into more than thirty languages. He is perhaps most well-known for his fiction series the Chronicles of Narnia, which alone have sold more than 100 million copies.

Serenity Prayer

God, give me grace to accept with serenity
The things that cannot be changed,
Courage to change the things
Which should be changed,
And the Wisdom to distinguish
The one from the other.
Living one day at a time,
Enjoying one moment at a time,
Accepting hardship as a pathway to peace,
Taking, as Jesus did,
This sinful world as it is,
Not as I would have it,
Trusting that You will make all things right,
If I surrender to Your will,
So that I may be reasonably happy in this life,
And supremely happy with You forever in the next.
Amen.

REINHOLD NIEBUHR (1892-1971)

Reinhold Niebuhr, an American theologian of German descent, shared this prayer during a sermon in 1943, at the height of the war against Germany. Neibuhr was an outspoken opponent of Hitler and the Nazi regime. He wrote the prayer to give comfort to a nation that was sending its sons off into an unknown future. His prayer was taken up and included in booklets for chaplains and servicemen in 1944 to offer them a sense of peace and comfort as they headed to the battlefield.

Ironically, in the aftermath of the war, many German politicians quoted the prayer to inspire and comfort a broken nation. They erroneously attributed it to an ancient German writer, not realizing it was penned by an American pastor.

The Serenity Prayer was adopted in the 1940s by Alcoholics Anonymous cofounder William Griffith Wilson for inclusion in the organization's twelve-step program. The prayer became an integral part of AA and other programs to follow. As fitting as it is for those corporate prayers, it is also a deeply moving personal prayer of surrender and serenity.

Prayer of Dedication

Almighty God, our heavenly Father,
who art of infinite majesty and mercy,
by whose counsel and might the courses of the worlds
are wisely ordained and irresistibly established,
yet who takes thought of the children of men,
and to whom our homage in all our works is justly due:
We bless and praise Thee....

We pray for all the nations of the earth;
that in equity and charity their sure foundations may
be established; that in piety and wisdom they can find a
true welfare, in obedience to Thee, glory and praise;
and that, in all the enlargements of their power,
they may be ever the joyful servants of Him
to whose holy dominion and kingdom shall be no end.

PRAYER DEDICATING THE STATUE OF LIBERTY

The Statue of Liberty, given to the United States by France as a symbol of friendship, was dedicated on October 28, 1886, by President Cleveland. Amidst the pomp and ceremony that accompanied the dedication service, including the city's first ticker-tape parade, Reverend Richard S. Storrs' prayer rang out across New York Harbor, praising Almighty God and petitioning that other nations be added to His kingdom.

The Soldier's Psalm

He who dwells in the shelter of the Most High
Will abide in the shadow of the Almighty.
*I will say to the L*ORD*,*
"My refuge and my fortress,
My God, in whom I trust!"
For it is He who delivers you
from the snare of the trapper
And from the deadly pestilence.
He will cover you with His pinions,
And under His wings you may seek refuge;
His faithfulness is a shield and bulwark.
You will not be afraid of the terror by night,
Or of the arrow that flies by day;
Of the pestilence that stalks in darkness,
Or of the destruction that lays waste at noon.
A thousand may fall at your side
And ten thousand at your right hand,

But it shall not approach you.
You will only look on with your eyes
And see the recompense of the wicked.
For you have made the LORD, my refuge,
Even the Most High, your dwelling place.

PSALM 91:1-9 NASB

This famous psalm is often referred to as the "Psalm of Protection" and also the "Soldier's Psalm." It remains a popular reading for servicemen and women, and many soldiers and service personnel often carry a copy of this Scripture with them when they are deployed into areas of armed conflict.

A Prayer for Sunday

It is right and our delight to give You thanks

and praise, Holy Father, living God,

Supreme over the world, Creator,

Provider, Savior, and Giver.

From a wandering nomad

You created Your family (Abraham);

For a burdened people You raised up a leader (Moses);

For a confused nation You chose a king (David);

For a rebellious crowd You sent Your prophets.

In these last days You have sent us Your Son, Your

perfect image, bringing Your kingdom, revealing Your

will, dying, rising, reigning, remaking

Your people for Yourself.

Through Him You have poured out Your Holy Spirit,

filling us with light and life.

FROM KENYAN LITURGY

It is well known that liturgy has had its part in church history, but we seldom recognize how many cultures have adopted the practice. This reading from Kenyan liturgy recognizes many of the main events throughout biblical history, reminding us that the importance of prayer is timeless and nationless.

A Blessing for Israel

Although you have been forsaken and hated,
with no one traveling through, I will make you the
everlasting pride and the joy of all generations.
You will drink the milk of nations and be nursed
at royal breasts. Then you will know that I,
the LORD, am your Savior, your Redeemer, the
Mighty One of Jacob…. No longer will violence
be heard in your land, nor ruin or destruction
within your borders, but you will call your walls
Salvation and your gates Praise.

Isaiah 60:15-16, 18 NIV

In 1844 Corrie ten Boom's grandfather Willem started a weekly prayer service in his home for the Jewish people and the peace of Jerusalem, based on Psalm 122:6, "Pray for the peace of Jerusalem: 'May they prosper who love you' " (NKJV).

These meetings were continued by Corrie's father, Casper, and were still taking place one hundred years after they began when their family was arrested for harboring Jews.

Willem's prayers for God's chosen ones continue today with the Corrie ten Boom Fellowship, a nonprofit organization that prays for the peace of Jerusalem and encourages Christians to exercise their faith by helping the Jewish people.

Leadership Blessing

We look gratefully to the past, and thank You that from the very foundations of America You granted our forefathers courage and wisdom, as they trusted in You. So we ask today that You would inspire us by their example; where there has been failure, forgive us; where there has been progress, confirm; where there has been success, give us humility; and teach us to follow Your instructions more closely as we enter the next century.

Give to all those to whom You have entrusted leadership today a desire to seek Your will and to do it.

William (Billy) F. Graham, an ordained Southern Baptist minister, became a household name when he began conducting crusades across the United States in the late 1940s. His crusades and sermons are still broadcast; his estimated lifetime audience has reportedly topped two billion. Graham is well respected internationally and has served as spiritual advisor for several US presidents.

Christmas Eve Prayer

Give us, O God, the vision which can see Your love in the world in spite of human failure. Give us the faith to trust Your goodness in spite of our ignorance and weakness. Give us the knowledge that we may continue to pray with understanding hearts. And show us what each one of us can do to set forward the coming of the day of universal peace.

FRANK BORMAN (1928-)

On Christmas Eve, 1968, the first manned mission to the moon entered lunar orbit. That evening, Commander Frank Borman's Christmas Eve prayer was given in a live television transmission, broadcast from lunar orbit showing Earth and the moon from Apollo 8. The other astronauts on the flight were Command Module Pilot Jim Lovell and Lunar Module Pilot William Anders. Commander Lovell said, "The vast loneliness is awe-inspiring, and it makes you realize just what you have back there on Earth." They ended the broadcast with the crew taking turns reading from the book of Genesis.

Seasons of Life

To every thing there is a season,
and a time to every purpose under the heaven:
a time to be born, and a time to die;
a time to plant, and a time to pluck up that
which is planted;
a time to kill, and a time to heal...
a time to weep, and a time to laugh;
a time to mourn, and a time to dance...
a time to embrace, and a time to refrain from embracing;
a time to get, and a time to lose...
a time to rend, and a time to sew;
a time to keep silence, and a time to speak;
a time to love, and a time to hate;
a time of war, and a time for peace.

ECCLESIASTES 3:1-8 KJV

Ecclesiastes has had a profound influence on Western literature. American author Thomas Wolfe called it "the noblest, the wisest, and the most powerful expression of man's life upon this earth...the greatest single piece of writing I have ever known."

Pete Seeger wrote a song in the fifties that matched the chapter almost word-for-word. "Turn! Turn! Turn! (To Everything There Is a Season)" became an international hit in 1965 when it was performed by American folk band The Byrds. As the song spoke to a generation of Americans experiencing the Vietnam War, so the soothing cadence of the seasons captured in this biblical book continues to touch people three thousand years after it was written.

Start Right

God, let me start off today on the right foot by realizing that when I fully and wholeheartedly follow You and Your teachings, I can enjoy a freer, more gratifying, joyful, and complete life than is possible any other way. Forgive me my sins of foolish timidity and lack of faith in You and myself, and bind me together with my Savior, Jesus Christ, through the Holy Spirit.
In Jesus's name I pray. Amen

Jimmy Carter (1924-)

The thirty-ninth president of the United States, Jimmy Carter, is the only president to receive the Nobel Peace Prize after leaving office. In 2002 the Norwegian Nobel Committee awarded it to him "for his decades of untiring effort to find peaceful solutions to international conflicts, to advance democracy and human rights, and to promote economic and social development."

God's Examples for Blessing a Child

"This is My beloved Son, in whom I am well-pleased."

MATTHEW 3:17

"No weapon that is formed against you will prosper;
And every tongue that accuses you in judgment
you will condemn. This is the heritage of the servants
of the LORD, *and their vindication is from Me,"*
declares the LORD.

ISAIAH 54:17 NASB

God gave us the perfect example of a spoken blessing over His son—words of love and affirmation—before Jesus's ministry had even begun. God revealed the importance of the spoken blessing with the words He gave for Aaron and his descendants to continue to speak over the Israelites in Numbers 6:24–27.

God said His blessing will come about by putting His name on the Israelites. A blessing is speaking the Word of God. It is speaking over a child what God says about him or her. God's Word spoken over your children will empower them to prosper because we have His promise in Isaiah 55:11 that His Word will not return void.

Let Your Light Shine

Dear Jesus, help us to spread Your fragrance everywhere we go; flood our souls with Your Spirit and life. Penetrate and possess our whole being so utterly that our lives may only be a radiance of Yours. Shine through us and be so in us that every soul we come in contact with may feel Your presence in our soul. Let them look up and see no longer us but only Jesus. Stay with us and then we shall begin to shine as You shine, so to shine as to be light to others. The light, O Jesus, will be all from You. None of it will be ours. It will be Your shining on others through us. Let us thus praise You in the way You love best by shining on those around us. Let us preach You without preaching; not by words, but by our example, by the catching force, the sympathetic influence of what we do, the evident fullness of the love our hearts bear to You.

MOTHER TERESA (1910-1997)

Mother Teresa was a Roman Catholic nun and missionary who spent her life working with the destitute in India. She founded the Missionaries of Charity, which consists of 4,500 sisters in 133 countries.

Prayer of Jabez

Oh, that You would bless me indeed, and enlarge my territory, that Your hand would be with me, and that You would keep me from evil, that I may not cause pain!

1 CHRONICLES 4:10 NKJV

We know very little about Jabez. In a chapter brimming with ancient lineage, two verses turn the spotlight on one son: "Now Jabez was more honorable than his brothers, and his mother called his name Jabez, saying, 'Because I bore him in pain'" (verse 9 NKJV). The mini-biography of Jabez records God's response before moving on: "God granted him what he requested."

After *The Prayer of Jabez: Breaking Through to the Blessed Life* by Bruce Wilkinson was published in 2000, millions started repeating the prayer on a daily basis.

Blessing of Peace

Go forth now, into the world in peace;
be of good courage; hold fast to that which is good,
render to no one evil for evil;
strengthen the fainthearted; support the weak;
help the afflicted; honor everyone; love and serve the Lord.
And the blessing of God Almighty, the God who created us,
the God who liberates us,
and the God who stays with us throughout eternity
be with you this day and forever more.
Amen.

WASHINGTON NATIONAL CATHEDRAL BULLETIN

As prayer gatherings were erupting spontaneously in public and private across the nation after the devastation of 911, an interfaith service was also quickly organized and held at the National Cathedral in Washington, DC.

Held on September 14, 2001, the service included many prayers, songs, Scripture readings, a message from Billy Graham, and an address from President George W. Bush, along with heartfelt anguish as the assembly of all faiths called out to God with mourning hearts. The service was concluded with this blessing from 1 Thessalonians (5:13–22), led by Bishop Dixon.

What I Do in Anything

Teach me, my God and King,
In all things Thee to see,
And what I do in anything,
To do it as for Thee.

GEORGE HERBERT (1593-1633)

Herbert was a Welsh-born poet, orator, and Anglican priest who is believed to have been the most skillful British devotional lyricist. He wrote poetry in English, Latin, and Greek. He described his writing as a picture of his conflict to subject himself to his Master, Jesus.

Prayerful Greetings

"Gruss Got!"

This common greeting used in and near Austria means literally "God greets you." It is used as the accepted greeting for meeting a stranger or someone with whom you are not on a first-name basis.

"Good-bye"

The most common English farewell word is a contraction of "God bless ye," from the mid-1500s.

Postscript Blessing

The blessings of our Lord Jesus Christ
be upon your spirits.

PHILIPPIANS 4:23 TLB

Paul wrote his letter to the church in Philippi while he was in chains (1:13). Despite his circumstances, it is filled with everything you would find today in a letter to loved ones: thanksgiving for generosity, news of mutual loved ones, and sharing from the heart—his filled with joy and Jesus. An inseparable combination.

The Living Bible ends the book of Philippians after verse 20 with "Sincerely, Paul." Verse 23 is the end of the three-verse "postscript," Paul's final wish from jail for the ones he loved so much. It is a PS that can be added to any heartfelt letter or e-mail even today.

Doxology

Praise God, from whom all blessings flow;
Praise him, all creatures here below;
Praise him above, ye heavenly host;
Praise Father, Son, and Holy Ghost.
Amen.

THOMAS KEN (1637-1711)

The Doxology is a short hymn of praise used in denominations worldwide, often at the end of a worship service. The words are the last verse of a hymn by Thomas Ken, titled "Awake, My Soul, and with the Sun," written in 1674.